It is appropriate that *Luck of the Draw* is to be presented in Melbourne during 1986—International Year of Peace (IYP).

The United Nations, in declaring an International Year of Peace, intended 1986 to be a time when governments, community groups and individuals would take initiatives to further the cause of peace, disarmament and social justice, and to heighten public awareness of these vital issues.

Luck of the Draw, by reminding us of the legacy of war, can serve to strengthen our resolve for peace.

VICTORIA

International Year of Peace 1986

LUCK
OF
THE DRAW

ROSEMARY JOHN

Current Theatre Series
published by Currency Press, Sydney
in association with Playbox Theatre Company, Melbourne

CURRENT THEATRE SERIES

First published in 1986 by
Currency Press Pty Ltd,
P.O. Box 452, Paddington, N.S.W. 2021,
Australia, in association with the
Playbox Theatre Company, Melbourne.

National Library of Australia card number and
ISBN 0 86819 145 0

Typeset and printed by Bridge Printery, Sydney

Publication assisted by the Literature Board of the Australia
Council, the Federal Government's arts funding and advisory
body.

Luck of the Draw was first performed by the Performing Ensemble of the Murray River Performing Group in the Wodonga Theatre, on 3 July 1985, with the following cast:

RICHARD	David Ogilvy
DIANNE	Lynne McGranger
JOHN	John Walker
KHAN	Tran Minh Nam
DANCER	Vincent Vaccari
SUSIE	Rosemary John

Directed by Phil Thomson
Original music by Al Mullins

CHARACTERS

RICHARD, a Vietnam Veteran, aged thirty-seven
DIANNE, Richard's wife, aged thirty-five
JOHN, Vietnam Veteran, Dianne's brother, aged thirty-seven
KHAN, a Vietnamese refugee, in his early twenties
DANCER, a black marketeer and con-man, in his early forties
SUSIE, a barmaid

SETTING

The stage is divided into four levels. The highest is John's bedroom. The second level, stage left is the dining area and front door; centre stage is the lounge area with stereo, etc.; stage right, the lowest level, is a bar.

The bar area is used as part of the house, except in scenes five to nine, where it becomes a pub.

ACT ONE

SCENE ONE

Late at night. RICHARD *enters front door, just home from the pub. He is drunk.*

RICHARD: About turn! Left right left right. I'm pissed, really pissed. Halt. One step forward. The training you receive in the army will be of benefit to you when you return to civilian life. Bullshit!

[*He gets a beer.*]

. . . I was in Vietnam . . . I chopped off ears and sent them home to my wife.

[*He laughs.*]

Nah . . . just kidding; I sat around in the rain . . . War is hell. Hell! War is rain! One big red stinking mud puddle . . . Rain, full of creeping, crawling, flying things . . . noise, artillery . . . thunder . . .

[*He laughs.*]

Hey! Guess what? . . . It's still raining! All personnel coming to Vietnam must first learn how to swim! . . . Tinea eating away at your feet, red, bloody, raw . . . shh! . . . shh! . . . Oh Jenny, Jenny, Daddy's told you this story a thousand times . . . Once upon a time—it wasn't raining— Daddy is standing by this road and along comes an old Vietnamese man with a long, grey, whispy beard and he's on a very rusty bike . . . squeak, squeak . . . and on the bike are three little girls, propped front and back, all dressed in white gauze . . . giggling and laughing. Tring, tring goes the bicycle bell . . . tring, tring and they're all waving . . . the sky is blue with white clouds and I can still feel . . . happy . . . but I haven't felt that since . . .

[RICHARD *looks at an empty spot on the sideboard. Pause. He starts to search through drawers and cupboards, throwing papers and photographs everywhere.*]

Where is it, where's it gone . . . ? Where's my little girl? Where'd the stupid bitch put it?

[DIANNE *appears in the doorway.* RICHARD *sees her.*]

Where's Jenny's photo?

[*He lurches towards her, knocking something over.*]

What have you done with it?

DIANNE: What's going on?

[*She starts to pick up some of the papers and photos.*]

RICHARD: Where is Jenny? Where is she?

DIANNE: It's all right . . . Come to bed.

[*She goes to put her arms around him.*]

RICHARD: [*pushing her away*] Get your hands off me . . . Where's my baby?

DIANNE: It's late. Come to bed, darling; come on.

RICHARD: Don't you tell me what to do . . . Where is she?

[*Silence.*]

Answer me.

[*Silence.*]

Are you deaf?

DIANNE: Please, love, leave it till the morning.

RICHARD: I am talking to you — about the photograph of my little girl who waits for her daddy to say goodnight to her.

DIANNE: I put it away. It only upsets you.

RICHARD: You've got thirty seconds to bring me that photo.

DIANNE: Richard, please!

RICHARD: Twenty-five seconds . . .

DIANNE: It hurts me to see you like this.

RICHARD: Nineteen . . . eighteen . . . I can't see it . . . it's not coming any closer. Why do I feel that no one is listening to me and that no one cares . . . ten seconds . . .

[*He grabs* DIANNE.]

DIANNE: Keep away from me.

[*He shoves her against the wall and holds her.*]

RICHARD: I don't want to hurt her again . . . Just want to know where she is . . . that's all . . .

DIANNE: I love Jenny, too. But she's gone.

RICHARD: She may be, but I'll never forget her.

DIANNE: Richard, don't do this to me . . . please don't bring it all up over and over again . . . I love you . . .

[*She puts her arms around him.*]

RICHARD: I'm sorry. Don't want to hurt you.

DIANNE: You have to understand, love, it's not good for you. John says it's unhealthy, you treating that photo like it's real.

RICHARD: So little Dianne and brother John have been talking about me behind my back. [*Mimicking* JOHN] It's not normal, Dianne, for your husband to remember his little girl. I resent that. Where does he come off? I'm sick and tired of John this, John that! I don't give a shit what John says. Who does he think he is? The ambassador from God? I'd like to punch him in the fucking mouth . . . Well, well, well . . . now what do we have here . . . John's precious coffee table . . . I don't think I like what that does to him.

[*He upturns it.*]

So he expects me to forget, does he? But it wasn't his kid, was it?

[RICHARD *throws and upturns furniture.*]

And what about this? [*Pointing to a piece of furniture.*] And this, and this.

[*He continues to upturn furniture.*]

DIANNE: That makes you feel better, does it? Ripping the house apart?

RICHARD: Don't talk to me like a kid . . . it's not your bloody house. It's your bloody brother's house. Why did you tell him that I talk to her? To me that's bloody bad taste. It's private!

DIANNE: I'm not fighting with you anymore.

[*She turns to go, but* RICHARD *grabs her.*]

RICHARD: You're not leaving this room till you give me back my photograph.

[*She shakes him off, gets the photo from a drawer and thrusts it at him.*]

[*holding the photograph to him*] And don't you ever talk to him about this, because . . . God I love her.

[DIANNE *stares at him, then walks out.* RICHARD, *now alone, stares at the photo.*]

You're the only one who understands . . . I can see it in your eyes . . . You have met the beast and passed through its shadow.

SCENE TWO

Seven am to eight am. The lounge room is still in utter chaos. JOHN *enters the front door, home from a late night of partying.*

JOHN: [*singing*] Happy birthday to me, happy birthday to me . . .

[*He looks around.*]

What the hell's happened here? Bloody Richard, I bet!

[*There is a knock at the door.*]

Now what?

[*Another knock.*]

All right, all right . . . I'm coming.

[JOHN *opens the door and sees* KHAN *holding a piece of paper.*]

No, I won't sign for it. I'm not buying anything and I don't believe in God. Piss off.

[*He slams the door and shakes his head in disbelief.*]

Now I'm seeing nogs everywhere. Must have had too much last night.

[*There is another knock.*]

Shit!

[*He opens the door.*]

I thought I told you to piss off. We don't want any. We've got enough.

KHAN: Excuse me, is Richard here?

JOHN: Eh?

KHAN: Richard Donally? Photographer? I'm Khan.

[KHAN *puts his hand out.*]

JOHN: Sorry, don't know him.

KHAN: He lives here?

[*Pause.*]

JOHN: He's gone away.

KHAN: When will he be back? Can I wait?

JOHN: Look, Nigel, you've got the wrong address. I live here . . . get it?

KHAN: [*looking at the piece of paper*] This is . . . Forty-four George Street?

JOHN: Yes.

KHAN: Has he moved?

JOHN: That's right, nog, and why don't you move off too?

[JOHN *tries to shut the door.*]

KHAN: Please . . . I understand . . . But it's all right. I know him . . . Will he be long?

JOHN: Look, I don't know. He didn't say. I don't know where he's gone.

KHAN: Is Dianne here?

JOHN: How do you know her?

KHAN: When Richard talking he says he has a wife, Dianne. You don't know when he comes back?

JOHN: I just said, I don't know.

KHAN: [*peering into the lounge room*] O.K. if I wait here?

    [*Pause.*]

I help you clean up.

    [KHAN *goes into the room, and picks up a chair.* JOHN *knocks it down again.*]

Please . . . He took photographs. He has photographs of my family. I am alone. He will help me. He will give me the pictures. I must see him.

JOHN: Well, he doesn't want to see you. He's gone away and why don't you? Back to your rice paddy.

    [KHAN *does not move.*]

There are two things that smell like rotten fish and only one of them's fish. If you don't clear off my property I'll call the police and get rid of the other. Understand? Didi Mao! I'll call the police!

    [*As* KHAN *moves outside, he slams the door.*]

Nog bastard.

SCENE THREE

Later. The lounge room is still a mess. DIANNE *sits drinking a cup of coffee.* JOHN *enters. He looks very unkempt. He looks around.*

DIANNE: You look how I feel . . . dreadful.

JOHN: Yeah, every time my heart beats my eyes go out of focus.

DIANNE: So what'd you do last night?

JOHN: Oh, had a few drinks . . . then a few more . . . and I end up going home with this beautiful sheila . . . but when I woke up she's old and ugly and has no teeth so I came home.

DIANNE: Not working today?

JOHN: If a man can't bludge on his birthday, when can he? What's all this about?

DIANNE: I put Jenny's photo away. You know what he can be like . . . He was raving on when he came home. I tried to calm him down but . . . he went crazy.

JOHN: So you gave the photo back?

DIANNE: Yeah.

JOHN: Well, I still think it's weird, having a photo of her playing in the water.

DIANNE: I hate seeing him this way. When he's depressed he talks about nothing but Jenny and when he's normal all he talks about is Vietnam. That war's biggest casualty looks like being our marriage.

JOHN: Trouble is, he sees that war through the bottom of a seven ounce glass.

[JOHN *gets a beer.*]

He's got to snap out of it. He can't wear a flak jacket all his life; shit, who does he think he is? Richard Donally, our very own Rambo!

[*Pause. He laughs.*]

DIANNE: What's so funny?

JOHN: Nothing.

DIANNE: Oh, come on, tell me.

JOHN: No . . . well this mess, this morning . . .

DIANNE: What about this morning?

JOHN: Nothing . . . it was nothing . . . oh, I dunno. It's just that all this mess reminds me of this one time when Pixi and I went into this bar in Vung Tau. Shit! I remember it . . . like it was yesterday. See, we're having a nice quiet drink talking about what was going on . . . y'know and the last thing we wanted was nog sheilas . . . annoying us . . . and this one over by the bar is going 'Whee Uc do loi! Me numbah one . . . boom, boom', and she comes charging along the bar and leaps into my lap and grabs me. I said, 'Don't keep it up nog, piss off!' and then here she comes again, and as she leaps through the air, I get her mid-flight with my boot. Wham! She goes flying through the back wall, screaming, 'You bad man you numbah welve, you numbah welve!' 'Piss off nog'. Then the pappa san, the big chief of the bar, comes wading in and tries to nail us and there's a punch up, so we threw him out the back in the rubbish bin . . . and every time he tried to get out, Pixi would push him back down, 'stay down there you nog bastard' . . . And then we broke the place up . . . Yeah, looked a bit like this.

DIANNE: Sometimes I wonder whose side you were on? I thought you went over there to help them.

JOHN: Sorry Di . . . just trying to cheer you up.

DIANNE: Thanks. Anyway, happy birthday, love. Give us a hug.

[*She hugs him.*]

I might as well get it over with . . . close your eyes.

JOHN: What's this?

DIANNE: Present time . . . now I didn't have much money . . . are they closed?

[JOHN *nods.*]

I really wanted to buy you something different.

[*She gets a bamboo plant and places it in front of him.*]

Da Da! Do you like it? I think it's great.

[JOHN *keeps his eyes shut.*]

C'mon, John, don't be an arsehole. Open your eyes.

[JOHN *opens them.*]

JOHN: It's a plant.

DIANNE: Isn't it beautiful?

JOHN: Umm! It's unusual!

DIANNE: You do like it, don't you?

[JOHN *stares at it. He starts to laugh.*]

JOHN: [*laughing*] Yeah. I really like it, but I can't help thinking of Richard waking up and seeing it!

DIANNE: Bugger Richard. It's yours! But you've got to look after it.

JOHN: It'll grow into a giant bamboo patch; it'll take over the lounge room. There'll be nowhere to sit. Did you buy this off a Vietnamese kid?

DIANNE: What are you going on about?

[*Pause.*]

I'm so stupid, aren't I? Does it bring back bad memories?

JOHN: Of course not. It doesn't bother me, but you know Richard, it might send him off. You know what we did with this stuff over there; made kites out of it. One time we made a kite out of bamboo about as high as this wall . . . Nah, you don't want to hear another story. [*Touching the bamboo*] Nah, this doesn't bother me.

[*He hugs her.*]

Thank you my love. So. [*Viewing the mess*] What are we going to do about . . . this?

DIANNE: I'm not touching it.

JOHN: Be buggered! I'm not cleaning it up.

DIANNE: Richard will clean it up.

JOHN: My, my, my! Haven't we changed? It's about time you stood up to him . . . Hey, tell you what: how about you and I go to the pub for a birthday drink and laughing boy can clean up the mess.

[RICHARD *walks in.*]

DIANNE: Speak of the devil.

JOHN: Hello!

DIANNE: You look like you just escaped from Hiroshima.

JOHN: He looks more as if he didn't!

[RICHARD *glares at* JOHN, *then stares at the mess.*]

RICHARD: What's all this?

DIANNE: This is your interior decorating.

RICHARD: What?!

DIANNE: You rearranged the furniture last night. I decided to leave it, so you could see what you did.

[*Silence.*]

I think we should talk about it.

[RICHARD *stares at* JOHN.]

RICHARD: O.K., then . . . Alone.

DIANNE: See you down the pub later.

JOHN: Yeah.

[*He looks at* DIANNE, *mouths 'be strong', and exits through the front door.*]

RICHARD: Look, I apologise. I honestly don't remember doing this. I can't explain.

DIANNE: Talk to me about it. For Christ's sake try and remember.

RICHARD: I don't need more of your bloody questions. It's not going to help. I'm going out for a drink. We can talk about it later.

DIANNE: You can't just walk out. You can at least clean up. I am sick to death of doing it for you . . .

RICHARD: All right, all right. Don't nag. Jesus Dianne. O.K. We'll clean it up.

DIANNE: No. You do it. You made the mess.

[*Silence.*]

Look, I want to help you, but I can't unless you let me.

RICHARD: What can we do? We're dead broke. I hate this town. I don't belong here, and since Jenny died I don't belong anywhere.

DIANNE: It's painful for both of us, but we're here and we have to try to get our lives together . . . You left the war behind when Jenny was born, you wanted to be with us, you showed us how much you loved us. You can't go on locking yourself in that bedroom for hours on end. You've got to forget Vietnam and you've got to forget Jenny. I know we've talked about this before, but we should have another child.

RICHARD: No!

DIANNE: It's been three years.

RICHARD: I don't want another one.

DIANNE: I do.

RICHARD: I'm not going to waste another bloody beautiful life. I'm not going to be the one who . . .

DIANNE: Stop it, Richard. You're blaming yourself, no one else is. It was an accident. For Christ's sake, love . . . it just happened that it was you there, not me.

RICHARD: I was sitting there by the pool . . . but I wasn't watching. I was . . . [*thinking about something else*] I'll never forgive myself.

DIANNE: Maybe we need a counsellor to help us . . . about Jenny, about the war.

RICHARD: How many times do we have to go over this? They don't know. They just read the little words in their little books . . . They're the blokes who didn't go. They waved the placards, played the guitars. There we are, seven thousand miles away and there's Dr Jim Bloody Cairns sitting in the middle of the road. No letters, no Christmas parcels: they're all piled up on the wharves because the fucking posties and wharfies didn't want to send them. And how did we feel? We felt bloody awful. They didn't care about us then and they certainly don't care now. Let's sweep it under the carpet, forget about it. All they care about are their cars, their jobs, where their next screw is coming from. I got one letter—one—in two months. I didn't ask to start a war with Vietnam, but I went because my marble came up in the lottery . . . but they didn't think about that when they stopped our fucking letters. Don't you see? Your letters were my link with you and my life here.

DIANNE: Sweetheart, that was fifteen years ago.

RICHARD: Listen to me: do you know what terrified me over there? That I missed you and my friends more than they missed me. I lost two years of my life; it was like I didn't exist. While I was there, all I wanted was to sleep in my house, watch my TV and walk down the street with my wife. I remember arriving at the airport thinking, 'I'm safe, they can't blow me up now'. We didn't expect cheers, we didn't want thank yous, but it was midnight, we were whisked away. We were an embarrassment, to be hidden, and fifteen years later we still are.

DIANNE: I love you very much, but I can't give you any more, I'm sorry. You have to change, take responsibility for yourself . . . I can't do that anymore, I'm leaving you here to clean up. I am only doing what you've been doing for fifteen years.

    [*She goes to the front door and exits.*]

Some time later. Loud music is playing. RICHARD *is trying to clean up.* JOHN *enters from his bedroom reasonably sober.*

RICHARD: Hi John. Sorry about all this. Happy birthday, mate. What did Dianne get you? It was a big secret. I couldn't look at it.

JOHN: A weird sort of present. Now don't laugh . . . I'll be most offended.

[JOHN *gets the plant from behind the chair.*]

RICHARD: It's a plant.

JOHN: Of course it's a bloody plant. So what do you reckon?

RICHARD: You don't like plants.

JOHN: It's the thought that counts.

RICHARD: It's a bloody ridiculous present.

JOHN: Why?

RICHARD: You don't want that.

JOHN: Why not? Why can't I have bamboo?

RICHARD: It's not the bamboo . . . Hell, I used to play with bamboo as a kid. I'd hang over the front gate with this long bamboo pole and threaten the kids going to Sunday School. 'Your money or your lives'. That was my Robin Hood phase . . . You were still into Noddy. Why don't you give it to someone else as a present?

JOHN: I'm not giving it away. Dianne gave it to me. It's special.

RICHARD: Yeah . . . you're right.

[*Long pause.*]

Di wants me to see a counsellor. I suppose I'll give it a go.

JOHN: You be careful who you go to: Rooter had a nasty shock. He went into group therapy with a squirrel doctor, and this bloke says to the nuts 'you have to find yourselves another life, a new life. Now, to help you do that, I want you to think of an animal and imitate it.' Now Rooter's battalion had a motto, 'Happy as pigs in mud', and he decides to be a pig. So all these blokes are whinnying like horses and barking like dogs, so he starts going oink, oink . . . shit this isn't for me and he oinks out the door as a pig never to return.

RICHARD: Thanks for the encouragement, mate.

JOHN: Nah, just warning you . . . Mind you, we had the right answer: sent him to a proper Vet counselling service. He seems to be getting on all right. He doesn't say g'day, he says g'd oink.

RICHARD: It's weird isn't it, the way things keep coming back.

JOHN: Look, mate, remember the good times. I just remember all the mad bloody things me mates did. Like one time Pixi had to dig up graves for the body counts, and he finds this brass jug. So he keeps it because he wants to take it home for a souvenir. Shows it to us at the canteen and fills it up with beer, and as he's drinking, he keeps saying 'this tastes real funny'. It wasn't till he was half way through that one of the blokes told him it was a Vietnamese burial urn!

[JOHN *laughs.*]

See, you're hung up on this guilt thing. But that was what your job was: to kill and to survive.

RICHARD: But what about the dreams? It's the dreams I can't stand . . .

[*Pause.*]

I'll wake up, the sweat's pouring off me . . . It's always the same one. I'm shaking so bad . . . I am sitting in this field and it's bright, with yellow flowers. I lie back, but as I look closer, they're not flowers . . . just grey rotting bodies, blowflies crawling in their eyes.

JOHN: Everyone has crazy dreams. It's not important; forget it. You become hard or you break. Don't think about it, O.K.?

RICHARD: O.K.

JOHN: Want a beer?

RICHARD: Thanks.

[*Long silence.* JOHN *studies* RICHARD *for a moment.*]

JOHN: How would you feel if someone from there turned up again? I mean a nog. What if a nog turned up and knocked on your door?

RICHARD: Don't be ridiculous.

JOHN: That's what I thought. But this morning there was this knock on the door, and guess what, it's Nigel nog and it's looking for you.

RICHARD: What did you do?

JOHN: Chucked him out.

RICHARD: This morning?

JOHN: Yeah.

RICHARD: Ah, come off it.

JOHN: I'm serious.

RICHARD: Why didn't you wake me?

JOHN: For a bloody nog?

RICHARD: You're telling me that a Vietnamese came here?

JOHN: Yeah, a nog and I told him to piss off.

RICHARD: For Christ's sake, it could have been important.

JOHN: Bullshit! Probably wanted to sell his sister. I don't know where he's been and that's why he wasn't coming in here.

RICHARD: What's so bloody special about here?

JOHN: Look mate, wait a minute. I own this house and if you don't like it you can get out now. I put up with with you and the crap you lay on my sister; if it's so important he'll find you or you'll find him. You're so bloody busy feeling sorry for yourself, you don't really give a shit about anyone . . . except this nog bastard you don't even know.

RICHARD: What's your problem? Eh, John? What gets to you? A Vietnamese comes to the door, why piss him off? What are you afraid of? Why do you hate them so much? How do you think they feel about us? Did you ever ask that? No, you'd never bother. They'd be better off if we'd never gone in there. Did the V.C. do any more damage than we did? We used the herbicides, defoliated, burned, bombed the place off the map—

JOHN: [*interrupting*] You bleedin' hearts give me the shits. I am sick of hearing you go on about the lost beauty of Vietnam.

RICHARD: You never even thought about it.

JOHN: Well, let me tell you something. It was a shit piece of dirt . . . nothing but rice paddies and jungle and now those slopes come over here . . . [*Pushing him*] Take our jobs, our homes; they're cunning. Animal cunning, that's what they are, animals. And for a fucking rice paddy my best mate got blown away, and it wasn't fuckin' worth it.

    [*He pushes* RICHARD, *hits him, then hits him again.* RICHARD *hits John in the mouth.* JOHN *staggers, holding his mouth. Long pause.*]

Shit this is a bloody great birthday I'm having . . . What are we doing? Fighting over some nog bastard . . . I should just go back to bed and start the day again. This is bloody incredible this is. John Evans, you have won this week's tatts lotto prize. And the lucky winner gets a nog! Your very own nog. We'll send him special delivery. But at the rate they're coming over we can all win one. If you call that winning, I don't, mate. Look, you and me go back a long way, but I'm not taking any more crap from you. So you clear this place up and I'll see you down the pub.

SCENE FIVE

Soft music plays. DANCER *sits at the bar.* SUSIE *serves him.*

DANCER: Scotch . . . Never mind the glass, I'll take the bottle.

[*He laughs.*]

You're really pretty; you brighten this place up. What's your name?

SUSIE: Susie.

DANCER: Well, Susie, they call me Dancer. Real quick on my feet. I'm a real good dancer. I've got natural animal rhythm; won a lot of cups and ribbons, but there's no money in it. Did anyone ever tell you, you look like an angel? How about going out with me when you finish up here . . .? Show me the town? Tell you what, we've got the place to ourselves . . . Turn the radio up.

[SUSIE *turns the music up.* DANCER *laughs.*]

Good music. Now, you play your cards right . . . you can have me. Here, buy yourself a drink.

[*He places $20 on the bar.* DIANNE *enters.*]

DIANNE: Hi, Susie.

SUSIE: Hi . . . What brings you here so early?

DIANNE: Richard.

[DIANNE *starts to play darts as scene progresses.*]

He got pissed last night and I left him to clean up the house.

SUSIE: Good on you, darl! Us women have got to stand up for ourselves, or there's no telling what'll happen.

[SUSIE *glances at* DANCER.]

DANCER: [*to* SUSIE, *confidentially*] Who's the lady?

SUSIE: She's married.

DANCER: C'mon, Susie. Is she a friend of yours? I'm getting lonely. I'm getting depressed. I think I'll trade you in for the blonde.

[DIANNE *finishes her darts and sits at a table.*]

SUSIE: You're on.

DANCER: So, what's her name?

SUSIE: Why don't you ask her?

DANCER: Introduce me.

SUSIE: Oh, no, you should do that . . . Show her some of that animal rhythm.

[DANCER *crosses to* DIANNE.]

DANCER: Since I'm the third of a threesome, I'd like to introduce myself . . . Dancer.

DIANNE: Dianne.

DANCER: Really? I've got a sister called Dianne.

DIANNE: I've got a reindeer called Dancer. Look, if you don't mind, I'd rather be by myself. I'm not real good company at the moment. Can I have a drink, Susie?

DANCER: Let me buy you one.

DIANNE: No, thanks . . . Look, I'm married.

DANCER: That's all right, that's fine. You see, I travel a lot — that's my business — and every pub I go into, I like to have a chat with someone.

DIANNE: I understand . . . I just don't want to talk.

DANCER: I've got the very thing. You're feeling depressed, right?

DIANNE: You could say that, yes.

DANCER: Well, I am going to get you a drink, the best drink around. [*To* SUSIE] Do you know how to make a Little Princess?

SUSIE: Yeah. Give her a little prince.

DANCER: [*crossing to the bar*] It's a drink . . . One ounce of white rum, an ounce of sweet vermouth. [*To* DIANNE] Now, this is guaranteed to get you out of a depressed mood.

DIANNE: It sounds terrible . . . and you sound crazy.

[SUSIE *pours the drinks out.* DANCER *takes them across to* DIANNE.]

DANCER: Crazy? Yeah, I am actually. I got dropped on my head as a kid and I never recovered. There we are now. This is guaranteed.

DIANNE: I don't think I want it.

DANCER: Go on, try it; you'll love it. It's a drink fit for a Princess. Hey! Princess Di!

[DIANNE *tastes it.*]

DIANNE: That's nice.

DANCER: Yeah! You see?

[DIANNE *starts to gulp the drink.*]

No! You just sip it. You don't want to get absolutely rotten, do you?

[DIANNE *nods.*]

Oh, well, in that case, throw the lot down and we'll have another one, O.K.? It's my shout.

[*They drink.*]

Susie, Princess Di would like the same again . . . and one for you, too.

SUSIE: Ta.

DIANNE: So, what do you do?

DANCER: I was a professional dancer all over the country. I'll teach you a few quick steps, if you like, your highness . . .

[DANCER *rises and begins to dance with a barstool.*]

The Riverina Rhumba!

[JOHN *enters, bleeding from the mouth.* DANCER *stops dancing and moves to the bar.*]

JOHN: Hey, Di . . . on the piss, are you? I'd be on the piss too, if I was married to that husband of yours.

SUSIE: If you were married to that husband of hers, you'd be in bloody gaol.

[DIANNE *sees* JOHN's *mouth.*]

DIANNE: Oh, Jesus! What happened?

JOHN: Your husband, that's what happened, love.

DIANNE: Susie, have you got some Dettol or something?

JOHN: A scotch'll do, Susie. Give us a kiss.

DIANNE: Why didn't you stop and put something on it? It looks awful.

JOHN: Don't fuss, Di . . . I'll just have a couple of drinks. Morning, Susie. Happy birthday, John. Thanks, Susie. Thanks a lot for the present. It's great.

SUSIE: Happy birthday, John. [*Pouring him a drink*] Here's a birthday treat . . .

JOHN: [*taking the drink*] This one's on the house is it? Good heavens!
[*He goes to* DIANNE's *table.*]

DIANNE: What happened?

JOHN: He jobbed me in the middle of the lounge room. Some fish-head turns up at the door and he jobs me.

DIANNE: What?

JOHN: I open the door this morning and there's the Viet Cong staring me in the face.

DIANNE: Slow down . . . Some Vietnamese turned up at the door. How many?

JOHN: Only one. He was looking for Richard, or so he said. I told him to piss off.

DIANNE: What did he look like?

JOHN: What do you mean, 'What did he look like'? They all look the same and smell the same. Like rotten fish. Anyhow, he hit me.

DIANNE: The Vietnamese hit you?

JOHN: Look, are you listening to me? Not the fish-head, the dick head! He comes up to me, grabs me by the hair — this is on my birthday mind you.

DIANNE: So he hit you first.

JOHN: Yeah . . . Well, we had a bit of a scuffle, then we both realised how
  ridiculous it was.

DIANNE: Oh God love, I'm sorry.

JOHN: Look, it's not your fault . . .

DANCER: Susie . . .? A double scotch.

  [SUSIE *prepares a scotch.*]

JOHN: [*looking across at* DANCER] Who's this, anyway?

DIANNE: This is Dancer. [*To* DANCER] My brother John. [*To* JOHN]
  Dancer.

  [JOHN *nods his head.* DANCER *takes the scotch and crosses to their
  table.*]

DANCER: [*passing the scotch to* JOHN] This is on me. I'm flush at
  the moment. I believe it's your birthday.

JOHN: Yeah! How are you? Good on you!

DANCER: How are you, mate? Is the other fella all right? I hope he
  looks worse than you do.

DIANNE: The other fella's my husband.

  [*They all laugh.*]

Anyhow, happy birthday, John.

  [*They all raise their glasses and drink.*]

DANCER: I know how you feel, John, about the Vietnamese. I was there
  too.

DIANNE: Oh, Gawd!

DANCER: Funny thing, actually; I've just come down from Sydney. I
  met a mate, and he says, 'Let's go for a meal.' He takes me to this
  Vietnamese restaurant and I say, 'What are you doing, bringing me
  in here?' 'It's good food,' he says. And then he says, 'what sort of wine
  do we have with dog?' 'Well, with dog,' I said, 'you have Woof Woof
  Blass.'

  [DANCER *laughs. The others remain silent.*]

You get it? Woof Woof Blass?

DIANNE: You've totally lost me.

JOHN: No, no; yeah, I understand.

DIANNE: [*standing*] I'll let you two get to know one another. I want a
  chat with Sue.

  [DIANNE *crosses to the bar.*]

JOHN: So you were over there, were you?

DANCER: Was I ever! All those beautiful girls!

JOHN: Yeah, but you could never relax, could you? You never knew what you'd catch! All the beautiful women had the clap. So I took all the ugly ones no one else wanted to root; that way I was safe. Some of my mates, though, they'd be out in the bush . . . pissing razor blades.

[JOHN *laughs.*]

You should have heard them. 'Oh! oh!' Dickhead, that's my brother-in-law, never got the clap either, but then all he did with the nogs was swap recipes . . . So what did you do?

DANCER: What did anyone do in Vietnam? It was convenient for me to take a holiday at the time. I had a bit of trouble with the taxation department, so I answered this ad in the paper and got a job with the Yanks, driving petrol tankers.

JOHN: So you were one of the ones who made money?

DANCER: I made my share. I'll tell you what happened. A couple of days after I got there, I was down at the docks. The Yank ships would dump their cargoes and leave. But instead of army supplies, I saw enough stuff to fill a million supermarkets. Radios, stereos and television sets; you name it! All sitting there! And the place was full of nogs going through the stuff, picking what they wanted and driving it away by the truckload. I thought to myself, 'Someone's making a lot of money here, so why shouldn't it be me? After all, I wasn't there for the freedom of the world was I? I was there to make a quid.'

JOHN: So you were in the black market?

DANCER: In a small way.

JOHN: Now, just let's get a few things clear, before we do any more celebrating. What were you selling? There was a lot of blokes over there, selling some pretty bad stuff to us at high prices. So what was your go? Were you one of the blokes who ripped us off, eh?

DANCER: Believe me, mate, I never ripped off a digger.

JOHN: So what did you sell?

DANCER: You are suspicious, aren't you? Look, mate, it hurt me too, seeing our blokes die. Now, there was penicillin. All the penicillin was kept for our blokes, but some of the empty bottles we filled with condensed milk and water. We'd sell that to the slopes. The stuff landed up in the North Vietnamese hospitals, so, indirectly, I killed off quite a few nogs myself.

[DANCER *laughs.*]

But I enjoyed myself.

DIANNE: [*to* SUSIE] So, what do you reckon, Susie?

SUSIE: I'd watch him if I were you. He thinks he's a real charmer, but he's a bit too smooth for me.

DIANNE: Yeah, he's slick, but he's good for a laugh and if I can handle Richard, I can certainly handle a travelling salesman. [*Calling to* JOHN *and* DANCER] Hey! You two! Time to break it up and join the party. Turn up the music, Susie . . . Let's liven this place up.

[SUSIE *turns the music up. All actors freeze on stage and the lights fade to blue.*]

SCENE SIX

RICHARD *cleans up the room with several photographs in his hand. He looks at the bamboo, then places* JENNY's *photograph against the plant.*

RICHARD: People say to me, 'You shouldn't take photos like that'; but it's got to be seen and remembered. I have to remember this piece of action, and that . . . Yeah I've got memories of all these pictures . . . [*Looking at a photograph in hand*] This one here? That's Davey . . . sun baking at Vung Tau. When we came back, we used to go spotlighting together every year, and one time he hid behind a tree, as a joke, didn't you, Davey? And out there in the dark, all I heard was the bang, bang of your tin. I whipped around, gun cocked. But I didn't shoot. I realised in time I was home. But sometimes . . . I think I'm back there. I did that day . . . with you, Jenny.

[*He looks at the photo against the bamboo.*]

You seemed happy in the wading pool, and the dog was by the fence, and I suddenly started thinking of this other dog, running towards us; a mangy red dog, running across the field . . . And as he runs, he leaves a trail of exploding mines and trip flares behind him . . . and we can't take our eyes off the dog as it comes closer, zig zagging across the field, and Smithy tries to shoot it and we're laughing because he's missed. Then Davey whispers, 'It's Charlie's dog. The V.C. are in there. They're in there.'

[*Pause. He finds it hard to go on.*]

I know you're in there, too, but I think you're safe. The water's shallow; but when I look, you're lying face down. I pick you up and put you down on the grass. Your little body . . . Your little body . . . Bodies everywhere, lying out on the mud. Stinking pile of flesh. Some shot in the head, others beaten with rifle butts, others hacked to pieces. I try to scream, and nothing comes out. I turn you over, pull the wet hair away from your eyes. You don't even cry. I hold you, but you're not there anymore.

[*He sits, head in hands. The lights fade to blue on the lounge and front door areas.*]

SCENE SEVEN

Lights go up on the pub. SUSIE *is revealed behind the bar with* JOHN *talking to her.* DIANNE *throws darts as* DANCER *watches. The darts game continues through the following dialogue.*

JOHN: I had this dream about you last night. See, we're lying on the bed and it's all furry and white, and you're in a leopard skin bikini . . .

SUSIE: Oh, listen to Tarzan.

[DANCER *tickles* DIANNE *and she misses the dart board.*]

Watch out for the paint work.

[JOHN *turns to look.*]

JOHN: That prick's got his hands on her again.

DIANNE: [*laughing, and looking across at* JOHN] I just hit my own number.

JOHN: Well you're not concentrating, are you?

DANCER: [*to* DIANNE] You're supposed to be looking at the board, beautiful.

DIANNE: [*to* JOHN] Your go. How many lives have you got left?

[JOHN *crosses to* DIANNE *and* DANCER.]

JOHN: [*taking the darts*] One . . . Watch this!

[*He takes aim.* DANCER *leans close to* DIANNE.]

DANCER: How about a kiss?

DIANNE: Forget it . . . Have a chip.

DANCER: Sorry, your highness.

[DANCER *tickles her.* DIANNE *giggles.*]

DIANNE: [*with a Pommy accent*] That's quite all right.

[JOHN *at last takes his shot.*]

JOHN: Shit . . . I missed.

[*He signals to* SUSIE *for another drink.*]

DANCER: [*to* DIANNE] Allow me to apologise to you.

DIANNE: [*with a heavy Aussie accent*] All right.

DANCER: By giving you a kiss.

> [DANCER *takes her and kisses her.* JOHN *goes to the bar to get his drink from* SUSIE.]

JOHN: This bloke went to the school of sleeze 'n squeeze. [*To* DANCER] That's my sister you're kissing. [*To* DIANNE] I'm driving you home.

DIANNE: Bullshit.

JOHN: Look, this is a family matter. I want to sort something out. Come here Dianne.

> [JOHN *takes her aside.* DANCER *takes the darts and starts to play.*]

Look, we're all friends, right? Now, how come I'm the one who everyone's killing? This isn't fair. [*Glancing at* DANCER*'s game*] What's his number? I'm going to get him.

DANCER: I got your number. You're out of the game.

> [*The darts game finishes.*]

JOHN: It's my birthday! I should win! Whose shout is it?

DIANNE: Yours. You are out of the game.

JOHN: Oh, thank you very much. Drinks all round, Susie — I feel dreadful. How about sleeping with me tonight?

> [DIANNE *goes back to the game.*]

SUSIE: Let's get this straight. Do you want a short term, no future, about a fortnight affair, or do you want a really deep and meaningful one night stand?

DANCER: She's too smart for you, John. 'Uc Doi Loi Cheap Charley.' Why don't you impress her with a Saigon Tea?

DIANNE: What's that?

JOHN: A shit soft drink the nog sheilas drank. They'd chuck it down their throats before you'd even got a couple of sips of beer. 'You numbah one; buy me another.' 'No way, noggie, it's your shout.'

> [*He laughs.*]

That's why all the whores called us Aussies, 'Cheap Charlies'. The Yanks spoilt them. Bloody useless, the Yanks. You know how I rate the American soldiers? Bad. Weak as piss. We were the number one soldiers over there. No, not soldiers: fighters, born fighters. We had individuality and initiative. We had contact drill; out on patrol, we knew where the machine gunner was, and every other bloke in the unit. We stood by one another. Mateship kept us going in the bad times. No one ever walked past anyone who was wounded, and if you did, it was only to throw a grenade. But those Yanks! Unbelievable! Bloody great ration packs on their back, lovely silver dog tags that blind Freddie could have

DIRECTOR'S NOTES

Rosemary's interest in the legacy of the Vietnam War prompted our Ensemble to begin looking at the situation of Vets in our region. The intensity of feelings we uncovered, and depth of the problems that still linger, had a profound effect on us all. Like many Australians we had almost forgotten Vietnam . . . soon we became aware of how, in our ignorance, we have badly treated our Veterans, and how far reaching the repercussions of the war still are.

For a nation which prides itself on its warriors, we met our returning Vets with a remarkable silence. As one regular soldier told us, 'there are no unwounded in any war', yet we have made it very difficult for our returning soldiers to heal themselves. Another Vet told us that the army only taught him how to 'dig holes and hide in them', and that this was no help to him in returning to civilian life. Perhaps he was wrong . . . for the first time in our history the Nation seemed to be saying to its returning soldiers 'dig yourself a hole somewhere and hide in it. We want to forget you and the war'.

Our research has taken us from the Sergeants' Mess at Latchford Barracks into Veterans' homes, to ANZAC Day breakfasts and to counselling services in Melbourne and Sydney. We read plentifully and listened attentively. The characters you will meet tonight are not based on specific individuals, but on an amalgamation of many. We trust that our audience will not read generalisations into our play, and assume all Vets are like Richard and John—each man we have met has had a different story, and most have managed to overcome their personal war legacies and are leading ordinary lives.

Whilst all the anecdotes and attitudes portrayed in the play are real, and have come to us first hand, this play contains a fictitious element, a 'What if?'. Rosemary has asked the question 'What if a Vietnamese refugee tracks down a Veteran he met during the war?' An unlikely event, we agree, but one which allows this play to look at the other Veterans of the war, our new community of Vietnamese refugees who remain mistrusted in their new home.

Luck of the Draw was written by using an exciting process which the Ensemble has developed over recent years. Rosie was given the use of the actors and director as creative tools with which to explore and work on her ideas. We helped her to develop scenes and bring characters to life. In this way she has written a play of great dramatic power which received plaudits from the public of Albury/Wodonga and our local Vietnam veterans.

Number seven of our Company objectives is 'to ensure that the original, innovative and nationally relevant work of the group finds avenues of expression beyond the region'. In recognising the merits of this production and sponsoring this season in Melbourne, the Playbox Theatre has provided an excellent avenue. We thank them for the opportunity to offer our work to you, the people of Melbourne.

Phil Thomson

WRITER'S NOTES

Luck of the Draw is a personal play. It came about because of a close involvement with a Vietnam veteran and the obvious disintegration of his personality as a result of his experiences in Vietnam.

A subsequent meeting with an Asian who had survived the same traumas, but from a different point of view, made me realise that this too was part of a story which needed telling and through that telling, hopefully, will enable the rest of us to understand a little better.

Luck of the Draw is an attempt to show the damage done by the 'forgotten war' to those by whom it will never be forgotten.

Rosemary John

The Murray River Performing Group

The Murray River Performing Group was formed in 1979 in response to local efforts to establish a professional theatre company in Albury/Wodonga. The performers, writers, technicians and office staff who make up the company strive towards the production and presentation of work which is original and innovative. It is also seen as vital that the Group's work is Australian and specific to our local community.

In its working structures and methods the Group attempts to reflect the collaborative nature of the theatre form. Whilst not denying the necessity for specialist skills we recognise the importance of co-operation. Therefore we believe that a collective structure in which each member of the company is empowered with responsibility for making decisions is essential.

We aim to produce a theatrical product of the highest standard which responds directly to the life and spirit of Australia. By utilising a wide variety of styles and venues the accessibility of the work is ensured.

In seven years the M.R.P.G. has produced some fifty original productions that have played to over three hundred thousand people and employed one hundred and fifty theatre workers. The work has ranged from serious drama through theatre restaurant, comedy, cabaret, community events and circus, and embraced the establishment of subsidiary groups such as the Leapers acrobatic troup and Bubu Yellul Aboriginal Dancers.

Whilst the core of the Group is our theatre wing, the Performing Ensemble, we also produce the Flying Fruit Fly Circus. The circus has twice toured internationally, becoming recognised as the world's best kids circus, and has twice been host to trainers from the Nanjing Acrobats of China.

The M.R.P.G. has, through constant hard work and dedication to its ideals, built a following in the Albury region that, in terms of percentage of population, would be of envy to any other performing arts company in Australia.

Now consolidated in a new headquarters the company is expanding its horizons. A National Circus School is planned which (politicians willing) will ensure the rebirth of Australia's acrobatic arts and the furtherance of the Fruit Flies' uniquely successful collaborative training and educational methods. We also seek to create more works of national significance and tour them further afield. A revamped production of our highly successful theatre restaurant play *Around the Bend* will soon tour the Murray River. We have several exciting and innovative productions on the drawing board and look forward to the next seven years.

THE MURRAY RIVER PERFORMING GROUP LTD.

Board of Directors

Bob Carr
Natalie Dyball
Kath Davey
Rosemary John
David Lester
Linda Moscrop
Cathy McGowan
Robert Perrier
George Prince
Barry Rogers
Jim Saleeba
Tony Smith
Phil Thomson
Chris Welsh — Chairperson

The Performing Ensemble would like to record here their appreciation and thanks for the hard work this group has put in.

The M.R.P.G. is funded by The Australia Council, Victorian Ministry of the Arts, Minister for the Arts in N.S.W., Albury City Council, City of Wodonga and the Albury/Wodonga Development Corporation.

609 Hovell Street, Albury, N.S.W. 2640
(060) 21 7433, 21 7615

The Playbox Theatre Company and
The Murray River Performing Group Ltd.

present

LUCK OF THE DRAW

by Rosemary John

RICHARD	David Ogilvy
DIANNE	Lynne McGranger
JOHN	John Walker
KHAN	Khiet Hoang
DANCER	Vince Vaccari
SUSIE	Rosemary John
DIRECTOR	Phil Thomson
ORIGINAL MUSIC	Al Mullins
SCRIPT EDITOR	Patrick Amer
SET DESIGN	David Ogilvy, Rob Connell
LIGHTING DESIGN	Naomi Stevenson, David Ogilvy
SOUND OPERATOR	Al Mullins
LIGHTING OPERATOR	Naomi Stevenson
PROPS & COSTUME	The Ensemble
PRODUCTION ASSISTANCE	Louise Salome
SET CONSTRUCTION SUPERVISORS	Colin Orchard, Phil Blakeley

The Murray River Performing Group would like to thank the following for their help during the production of *Luck of the Draw*:

The Border Vietnam Vets Association
Vet Counselling Services, Melbourne and Sydney
The various individuals who trusted us with their personal stories
and all our community in Albury/Wodonga.
Flicks of Albury for hair design.

The Performing Ensemble acknowledges the support and assistance of the Lee Jeans Company who are also based in Albury/Wodonga.

First performance in Melbourne at the St Martin's Theatre
10th March 1986

vii

PHIL THOMSON *Director*

An actor, writer and clown as well as director, Phil has worked with many companies throughout Australia. He has directed for W.E.S.T. Theatre Co., Victorian College of the Arts, West Australian Theatre Co., 1-2-1 Theatre, C.A.T.S. and Nomadic Arts. His productions have toured New Guinea and most States of Australia. Phil was also awarded a Director's Development Grant by the Australia Council in 1983 and joined the M.R.P.G. at the beginning of 1984.

ROSEMARY JOHN *(Playwright) Susie*

Rosemary John, an actress/writer, joined the M.R.P.G. in 1984. She spent five years in America working with such companies as S.C.C.T., La Mama Hollywood, Missouri Repertory Theatre and D.P.I. Kansas City. *The Good Shepherd*, a play about child abuse, won her a top place in a U.S.A. nationwide Playwriting Competition. Rosemary is currently writing a play with Patrick Amer about vaudeville/circus star, Micky Ashton.

AL MULLINS *Music*

Al is the newest member of the Ensemble, and has been engaged as musician-composer in residence since June 1985. He is no stranger to the M.R.P.G. An original member of the Flying Fruit Fly Circus band the 'Rhythm Rats', Al is also the composer of scores for the M.R.P.G. productions *Strange Incarceration* (1983), *Bleedin' Butterflies* (1984) and *Around the Bend* (1984). Al left Albury in 1984 to work in Melbourne, but returned when offered full-time employment and what hard-up musician wouldn't.

KHIET HOANG *Khan*

Born in Saigon, Hoang trained as a Buddhist monk for two years after leaving school before managing to leave Vietnam by boat. After four months in Indonesia he came to Australia in 1982 with his father and two brothers. Mother and four youngest are still in Vietnam. Gaining his high school certificate, Hoang found various odd jobs while he worked with Smiling Teeth Youth Theatre in 1984 and 85. *Snap Shots*, a group-devised play about growing up in multicultural western suburbs, was performed in schools, community centres and the Seymour Centre for the Sydney Youth Festival.

LYNNE McGRANGER *Dianne*

After giving up teaching, Lynne joined the Q Theatre, Sydney, as a full-time acting student, having already received ten years' training in ballet and modern dance. Whilst at the 'Q' Lynne worked in a variety of productions ranging from pantomime to Shakespeare and from rock opera to traditional drama. Lynne has worked in television, Theatre in Education, Theatre Restaurant and worked with children and adults in theatre workshops. Lynne joined the M.R.P.G. in 1984.

DAVID OGILVY *Richard*

David gave up his banking career when he realised that regretfully the safe combination was indeed safe. He then spent several years at university to reject a teaching career and finally accepted a position with Arena Theatre in Melbourne. After leaving Arena nine months later he was invited to join the Australian Puppet Theatre for its European tour of Nigel Triffet's *Momma's Little Horror Show*. Upon his return to Australia David was offered a short-term contract with the M.R.P.G. to work in *Liquid Amber* in 1982. He has been with the M.R.P.G. ever since.

VINCENT VACCARI *Dancer*

Vincent Vaccari joined the M.R.P.G. in 1985. Multi-cultural and multi-skilled, at 36 he says he has done the unusual and the usual things actors do when not performing.

A graduate of the Australian National Memorial Theatre in 1974, Vince has worked in cabaret, appeared in the mini-series *Waterfront* and episodes of *A Country Practice*, a number of popular Melbourne underground comedy movies, numerous television advertisements, and in 1984, was a part of the very successful *A Fruitcake of Australian Stories*.

Alas, he will be leaving the M.R.P.G. in July, after the *Around the Bend* tour to resume work in film, get married and complete the renovations to his home in Fitzroy.

JOHN WALKER *John*

John is a former usher at the Playbox Theatre and a graduate of the Victorian College of the Arts Drama School. John's first professional part was with the M.R.P.G. in *Liquid Amber* in 1982. He then worked with the community theatre companies Theatre Works and Drama Project Trust in Melbourne, as well as performing traditional pantomimes with the Sydney-based Rainbow Management. He has been with the M.R.P.G. for the last two years.

THE PLAYBOX THEATRE COMPANY

The Playbox Theatre Company is a non-profit company receiving Federal and State support, with a permanent staff of twelve. At present it is a company without a theatre following the fire which destroyed our two performance spaces in Exhibition Street in 1984. Since then we have toured to venues throughout Melbourne including the Studio Theatre of the Victorian Arts Centre.

In the nine years since the Company was founded it has established itself as one of Australia's most innovative drama companies with a national reputation for creative daring. Our artistic policy is to present the best in contemporary theatre. We have performed over seventy Australian plays and presented Australian premieres of over thirty overseas plays. We have toured extensively throughout Australia and have hosted exciting work from interstate and overseas, including the Jiangsu Peking Opera and the Nanjing Acrobats from China and most recently The Medieval Players and Footsbarn Travelling Theatre from England.

With the appointment of James McCaughey as Co-Executive Director in 1985, the Company will look increasingly towards young Australian talent from all spheres of the arts.

Since the fire our energies have been directed towards finding a new home and we hope to be able to announce the address in the very near future.

If you would like to be on our mailing list phone (03) 634 888.

Administration 63 7643
Box office 63 4888
Temporary Office: Shop 32, Collins Place,
45 Collins St., Melbourne 3000

Board of Directors
Graeme Samuel (Chairman)
Tom Dery (Deputy Chairman)
Tony Adair, Barry Conyngham, Rhonda Galbally, Wendy Harmer,
Clifford Hocking, June Jago, Frank Mahlab, Jillian Murray,
Peter Maund, Jill Robb, Tony Staley

Executive Directors	James McCaughey Jill Smith
Writers-in-Residence	Julianne O'Brien Hannie Rayson
Composer-in-Residence	Richard Vella
Executive Assistants	Kim Bowen Birgette Engdahl Jo Litson
Box Office Manager	Clare Fleming
Publicity	Josephine Ridge
Production Manager	Yvonne Hockey
Stage Manager	Ross Murray
Construction Supervisor	Colin Orchard
Wardrobe Co-Ordinator	Frances Farmer
Photography	David Simmonds—Sterio Stills
Graphic Art	David Hughes Design

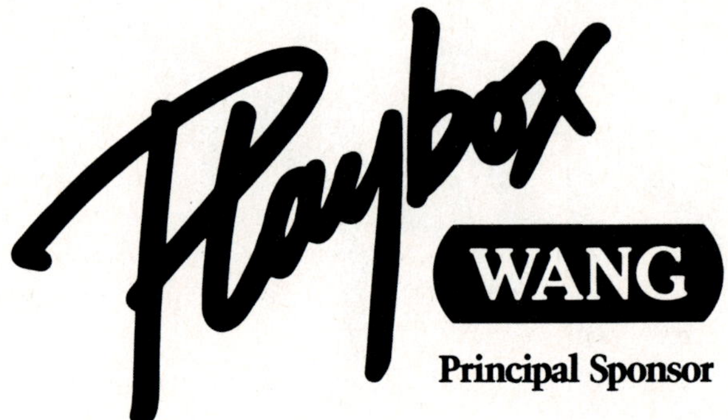

GRATEFULLY ACKNOWLEDGES
THE GENEROUS SUPPORT OF

The Board and Staff of the Playbox Theatre would like to thank

The Victorian Government through the Ministry for the Arts for a general grant.

The Theatre Board of the Australia Council (the Federal Government's arts funding and advisory body) for a general grant.

WANG Computer Pty. Ltd. for Technology, Marketing and Development assistance.

The Shell Company of Australia for sponsorship of the Studio Thoatre Programme at the Victorian Arts Centre.

C.R.A. Ltd., for rehearsal and storage area.

The Literature and Theatre Boards of the Australia Council for Playwright-in-Residence 1985/86 (Hannie Rayson) and 1986 (Julianne O'Brien).

Music Board of the Australia Council for Composer-in-Residence (Richard Vella).

The Theatre Board and Community Arts Board of the Australia Council, and the Victorian Ministry of the Arts for the secondment of John Paxinos whilst completing an M.B.A. at Monash University.

Mitchelton Vintners Pty. Ltd. for Premium wines for PLAYBOOK Patrons.

Brash Holdings — for Sponsorship of THE OATH OF BAD BROWN BILL.

Wilson Parking for donation of parking space.

Playbox artists choose Ndumsky of 372 Drummond Street, Carlton, for the best hairdressing in Melbourne. Phone: 347 1347.

seen in the moonlight, and their helmets covered in white insect repellent. They'd shoot at the rubber trees and at each other like they were in some bloody John Wayne movie. 'Hey guys, let's go for the kill.'

[JOHN *takes a drink.*]

The only ones I had any time for were their 'dust off' chopper pilots. They were bloody marvellous. Those helicopters would come flying through the thick jungle and get you out fast. There'd be a machine gunner at the door going bam bam bam [*making sound of gunfire*]. 'Throw smoke man . . . Throw red smoke, you Aussie bastards, we can't see you.' Then they'd lift you up fast . . . But they'd be there in ten minutes, wherever you were.

[*Silence. They all look at him.* JOHN *holds his glass out to* SUSIE.]

Fill her up, Susie.

DANCER: So, why did you leave the army?

JOHN: I only signed up for three years . . .

DANCER: What did you do then?

JOHN: I became a surveyor, didn't I? I got in trouble when I came back from Vietnam though — unbelievable! See, when I came back they were holding a moratorium, I was in Brisbane at the time, and there's bloody Jim Cairns leading the students. Well, we decided to hang a bit of dirt on those whackers. You know, have a drink at the Treasury Hotel and heckle them. Sure enough there are all those long-haired guys yahooing about this and that, and as they march, they gather people, who didn't know what the hell is going on, but joining in anyway . . . and outside the hotel there's a Vietnam veteran, with one leg blown off. He's got a walking stick and he's standing there on the footpath, shouting at them . . . then a couple of those bastards from the crowd come up and push him over. We run out of the pub and punch the shit out of them . . . believe me those blokes marching are too bloody scared to have a good go, they're screaming the odds . . . well it's one of those days when the TV crews were there . . . they don't show the poor bastard getting knocked over, just the punch-up, and that night on the news, my mug, with a split lip, is all over the screen. I got fourteen days confined to barracks, and those other bastards walked away laughing. The Vietnam Vets have always been treated like rubbish.

[*He goes to the bar.*]

Let's have a toast to my mates who went to Vietnam.
All of them were bloody mad.

DANCER: Let's have a toast to the ones who were smart enough not to get sent.

DIANNE: Well, let's not forget the ones who did go and did die. 'They shall not grow old as we who are left grow old. Age shall not weary them nor the years condemn. At the going down of the sun, and in the morning . . .'

[SUSIE *and* DIANNE *raise their glasses.*]

SUSIE:
DIANNE: } We will remember them . . .

JOHN: Hold on, what is this. A bloody ANZAC service? That's all very nice and sentimental, but that's about real wars where people cared. Vietnam wasn't a real war, and no one cared. You'd see a bloke with his legs blown off, and he's crying but you know no one out there cared. What did we get for giving our lives? What did we get when we came back home? We got spat on. We got blamed for killing those cunts, but we didn't know who the enemy were. Those bastards didn't put on uniforms like us. They'd plant rice all day and dig panji pits at night, pits filled with bamboo spikes that they'd shit on and piss on then camouflage as booby traps. They'd rig coils of barbed wire in the bushes, drawn tight so they would rip you across the balls when you tripped the wire. They hid in tunnels fifty feet below the ground, tunnels so small you'd have to crawl on your hands and knees to get in. If they're not V.C. today, they will be tomorrow, so why not kill them all, wipe their silly fucking smiles off their faces forever.

[*Lights fade on the front door and lounge areas. There is a knock at the door.* RICHARD *opens it to reveal* KHAN.]

KHAN: Richard? Richard Donally?

[KHAN and RICHARD *look at one another.*]

END OF ACT ONE

ACT TWO

SCENE ONE

KHAN *and* RICHARD *face each other.*

KHAN: Richard?

RICHARD: Yeah. Were you here this morning?

KHAN: Yes.

RICHARD: Come in.

KHAN: I am Khan. I always know that I will find you.

> [KHAN *pulls out a dog tag from around his neck.* RICHARD *looks at it.*]

RICHARD: Where did you get this?

KHAN: You gave it to me.

RICHARD: To you? . . . No, not to you . . . What's your name?

KHAN: Khan.

RICHARD: [*taking the dog tags*] Give me this. This is weird. I . . . I know you. [*Half crying, half laughing*] Come on, Richard, come on . . . There's the bridge . . . and all the little kids running around trying to sell us everything in sight.

> [KHAN *makes a fishing motion.*]

Richie fish . . . Richie fish . . . You're Captain Cook's son? Quan's son?

KHAN: [*smiling*] Fish. [*Making the fishing motion*] Take Richie fishing.

RICHARD: Oh God, I'm so sorry. You were just a little boy . . . and now . . . Trinh Khan! What on earth are you doing here?

KHAN: I've been looking for you. You remember me?

RICHARD: You're grown up.

KHAN: [*sitting*] Used to be little.

> [RICHARD *smiles.*]

You take pictures still?

RICHARD: Not any more . . . Not in the last few years.

KHAN: You take pictures of my family. I have nothing left. I came all the way to find you. You give pictures to me? I need to see them.

RICHARD: All right . . . Hold on, what happened to your family?

KHAN: My father die in war. They kill my mother, burn our house.

RICHARD: How long have you been looking for me?

KHAN: I come in '82. I know if I search long enough I will find you. That you will have pictures for me.

RICHARD: I have a lot of photographs of the war . . . but I don't know if the ones you want are here.

[RICHARD *goes to the sideboard and looks for the photos.*]

Are they really so important to you?

KHAN: In my country we worship ancestors. Now I have lost my family and my country. If you have pictures, then I am close to my family even though they are dead. They will always be with me because of your pictures.

[RICHARD *finds a box of photos and goes through it.* KHAN *watches him.*]

RICHARD: So how did you get out of Vietnam?

KHAN: I came on boat. We think it will only take a few days before we are picked up, but the ships ignore us. For fifteen days we have no water. We drink seawater, eat raw rice. Many die, but each day I say to myself 'you will live', and now that I am here, in this country, I know that to survive is everything.

[*Silence.*]

RICHARD: I remember. We were on a bridge. It was cold. I was trying to say goodbye to you, but all you said was 'when are you coming back?' I knew that I would never come back, but I didn't know how to tell you; so I gave you these. 'Keep these for good luck, remembrance, and hope.'

KHAN: Yes, I am here now. It is a happy day.

[RICHARD *has found the photographs.* KHAN *sees Jenny's photograph.*]

Is this your child?

RICHARD: Yes, but she's dead too. I think these are what you want.

[*He hands photos to* KHAN.]

KHAN: [*in Vietnamese*] Father, I am here. Can you see me?

[*Pause.*]

[*In English*] Please, I keep the pictures. Especially this one.

[KHAN *shows photo of him and* RICHARD.]

RICHARD: So that was me fifteen years ago. Was that how I used to be? Where did I get lost? Jesus, I've been a stupid bastard.

[*Lights fade to blue.*]

Lights go up on the bar area. DANCER *is telling the end of a joke.*

DANCER: He's had a great night, and in the morning he's leaving, and the German girl says, 'The Marks, what about the Marks?', and he says, 'Nine out of ten'.

[*They all laugh.*]

DIANNE: Whose shout is it?

JOHN: Where's my wallet?

DANCER: Tell you what: let me do it.

JOHN: Nah, you can't keep doing that.

[*He looks at his empty wallet.*]

Tell you what: I'll give you an arm wrestle.

DANCER: You'll give me an arm wrestle? All right. Left or right arm?

JOHN: Left. And the loser has to buy a double shout.

DANCER: You're on.

JOHN: O.K.?

DANCER: No cheating, right? Fair dinkum. You ready?

JOHN: You've got to put your other arm behind your back.

[*They start to arm wrestle.*]

DIANNE: Go Johnny . . . Go . . . Pissweak . . . Look at these men; they're supposed to be strong.

SUSIE: Yeah, bloody heroes, aren't they.

[DIANNE *stands behind* DANCER.]

DANCER: [*laughing*] Go away.

DIANNE: I'll tickle you.

[DANCER *laughs. She tickles him.* JOHN *pushes* DANCER's *arm over.*]

DANCER: That one's by default.

JOHN: All right. Dianne buys the drinks.

DANCER: Yeah.

DIANNE: I bought the last round.

JOHN:
DANCER: } [*together*] No, I did!

DIANNE: Bullshit.

JOHN: You stuffed up the game. Pay up.

DIANNE: [*to* DANCER] I want to arm wrestle you now.

[DIANNE *goes to sit on the chair but falls on the floor.* DANCER *pulls her back up. He keeps hold of her hand.*]

DIANNE: Let go of me.

DANCER: You're beautiful.

JOHN: What a load of crap.

[JOHN *goes to the bar.*]

DANCER: [*putting his arm on the table*] You ready?

DIANNE: I'm ready.

[*They arm wrestle.*]

DANCER: You're a tough one.

SUSIE: Come on, Di!

JOHN: Come on . . . Three double scotches ride on it!

DANCER: Come on . . . Push.

[*She grabs his hand with both hands and pushes it down. She laughs.*]
Cheat! One more time!

DIANNE: No, I can't . . . Let's go and buy a pizza; I need food. C'mon, Johnny, let's get something to eat. I'll get you another present.

[DIANNE *goes to* JOHN.]
You didn't really like the plant, did you? What about a dog?

JOHN: Why do I want a dog? Who's going to look after it?

DIANNE: Richard will . . . He might like a dog. I saw this TV programme where disturbed people became better if they had an animal around them.

[*He laughs.*]

JOHN: He already has. You are really pissed, aren't you? I can't take much more of this.

[JOHN *goes to exit stage right.*]

DIANNE: Where are you going?

JOHN: The dunny.

[JOHN *exits.*]

DIANNE: [*to* DANCER] He likes dogs.

DANCER: I thought he said he didn't want one.

DIANNE: Not John: Richard.

DANCER: So what's his problem?

DIANNE: John's?

DANCER: No; what's the matter with your husband?

DIANNE: He won't talk to people. If anyone comes around, he puts the headphones on and listens to the stereo. He never goes out, unless it's for a drink. He doesn't want to talk to our friends; sometimes not even to me. It's like I'm not there . . . And when he's drunk, he talks about the war.

DANCER: I understand that! I do! I don't respect people, present company excepted. You can buy them and you can sell them. You can turn anyone into a murderer, just give them a religion, or a flag.

DIANNE: I'm proud to be an Australian.

DANCER: All flags are garbage. All religion is garbage. They are all different languages for the word 'Kill'. See, Princess, you must learn, never underestimate the power of greed and the power of fear.

[JOHN *comes back in.*]

We're all killers.

DIANNE: I didn't understand a word of that. I think you'd get on with Richard. Why don't you come home and meet him?

DANCER: I'd like to.

[*He smiles.*]

That would be nice.

JOHN: What are you going on about now?

[DIANNE *starts to say something but* DANCER *jumps in.*]

DANCER: Di was saying how Richard has had enough of people. You know what? I feel like that sometimes. When I retire I'll build this huge house in the desert. It'll have a sauna, a swimming pool, courtyards with fountains and I'll put up a big wall all around it, covered in barbed wire. I'll keep trained Dobermans . . .

[DANCER *laughs.*]

Just to keep strangers out.

JOHN: I'd get a silver Porsche. Something to get the adrenalin going. The faster the better into that corner. It's like a woman—make her do anything. It'd be pure sex, mate, pure sex.

[DIANNE *groans.*]

DIANNE: Oh, don't start him him off on cars . . . Let's go and eat.

JOHN: I want another drink.

DIANNE: No! You've had enough. Time to go home. See laughing boy.

JOHN: Want to come by later, Susie?

SUSIE: Nah . . . I'll catch up with you another time.

JOHN: Yeah, tomorrow. Bye love. [*To* DIANNE] What are we doing? I'm broke.

DANCER: I'll buy the booze.

DIANNE: Port! A bucket of it. See ya Susie.

[*She exits.*]

DANCER: I'll buy some booze, then.

[*A slight pause.*]

JOHN: All right. See you outside.

[JOHN *exits.*]

DANCER: A dozen stubbies—and a couple of bottles of Port. How about you and me get together later on . . . You know, go out to a restaurant, have some Chinese food? Do you like Chinese food?

SUSIE: I thought you were going with them.

DANCER: Yeah, but you never know how these things turn out, do you?

[*The lights fade to blue on the bar area.*]

SCENE THREE

RICHARD *and* KHAN *are in the blue lights, with a flash camera on the upturned table.* RICHARD *takes a photo of* KHAN, *who then takes one of* RICHARD. RICHARD *sets the flash and rushes to the lounge for a photo of them together. As blues come up they start to clean the room.*

RICHARD: Your dad was real good scrub bashing, he came in very handy—could always find the booby traps. I remember when I got sick, he'd have this medicine and rub it across my forehead. God, that stuff would go right through your head, then he'd pinch my forehead [*he shows* KHAN] right here between the eyes, and pinch it hard, to pull out the evil spirit.

KHAN: And did it work?

RICHARD: Yeah! but sometimes I ended up with a nasty bruise.

[*He laughs.*]

The other blokes thought I was crackers. Give us a hand with this.

[*He moves the couch.*]

You're doing a great job. When we put the decorations up John won't even know this place. Would you like another cup of tea?

KHAN: No thanks, I still have some left.

RICHARD: So things weren't that good after the war?

KHAN: No, a lot of people not happy with the new Government. It is controlled by the North Vietnamese. They don't want the Viet Cong to be in government too. They don't want them to have power. They say go back to your villages, go back to where you belong. But there were some strange stories. Once, North Vietnamese soldier comes into hotel and sit in foyer. And he saw a man walk into the lift. The door of the lift close. He is very surprised. He has not a seen a lift before. A few minutes time, the door of the lift opens and a lady comes out. He is very surprised 'Oh God! This machine is wonderful, it change a man into a woman!'

[RICHARD *and* KHAN *laugh.*]

You like that? I tell you another. This also happen in a hotel. Once a North Vietnamese soldier bring vegetable back into hotel room. He take it into bathroom. He see toilet there. He didn't know this was a toilet. I think in his life he never see this before. The soldier thought this was a sink to clean the vegetables in, he didn't know where the water come from. He look around and sees button on top. He press and all the vegetables gone! And he sulks! 'This machine has stolen all my vegetables!'

RICHARD: Would you ever go back?

KHAN: No. I have made Australia my home . . . even though many do not make us welcome . . . like John . . . he is very angry this morning.

[KHAN *and* RICHARD *put a happy birthday banner around the bar and hang ribbons from bottles. The bamboo plant is placed on the far end of the bar.*]

RICHARD: Oh . . . he just gets that way sometimes. Don't worry . . . you caught him at a bad moment. He had a hangover.

KHAN: Will you come and see me in Melbourne?

RICHARD: Yeah. Of course I will.

KHAN: You can stay with me in our flat.

RICHARD: O.K. I'd like that.

[*He brings a bottle of wine and opens it.*]

Now we have to let this breathe.

KHAN: Breathe?

RICHARD: Gets rid of the acid . . . Would you like a taste? Have a sip.

[RICHARD *gets* KHAN *a glass and fills it.* KHAN *sips. Pause.*]

What do you reckon?

KHAN: I don't think it breathes.

[RICHARD *takes the glass and tastes it.*]

RICHARD: Mmm! You're right there! I don't think it's breathed for a long time. It's pretty putrid.

[*Noises of the three coming home are heard, off.*]

DIANNE: [*off*] We're home, Richard.

JOHN: [*off*] Here! That's my hand you've got a hold of!

DANCER: [*off*] Sorry, mate.

RICHARD: [*to* KHAN] Shit! Sorry! Tell you what . . . John may be a little uptight. Why don't you go into the kitchen? Make yourself a sandwich for the train trip, O.K.? That'll give him time to settle down. You know where everything is.

KHAN: O.K. I'll make sandwich: vegemite; I like it very much.

RICHARD: Just help yourself.

[DIANNE *opens the door a crack.*]

DIANNE: You won't believe this! It's spotless! He's cleaned the place up and decorated it! Oh Richard!

JOHN: [*off*] Let's see. [JOHN *pushes past her into the room.*] It's bloody amazing.

[DANCER *enters and looks around.* DIANNE *rushes over to* RICHARD *and throws her arms around him.*]

DIANNE: It's absolutely wonderful, sweetheart.

[*She kisses him, then turns to* DANCER.]

This is Dancer. We met him in the pub.

DANCER: Pleased to meet you, mate. Heard a lot about you!

RICHARD: Oh yes? Good or bad?

[DANCER *walks past him.*]

DANCER: What do you reckon?

DIANNE: He's just passing through town.

RICHARD: [*to* DANCER] You can stay to dinner; there's plenty.

[JOHN *goes behind the bar.*]

JOHN: [*to* DANCER] Pull up a stool. Let's have a beer. [*To* RICHARD] Bloody good, Richard, bloody good.

[DANCER *sits at the bar and* JOHN *makes comments to him about the bamboo.*]

DIANNE: I'm very proud of you, sweetheart.

RICHARD: Di . . . Listen, it's important. I have to talk to you.

DIANNE: All right, my love. John, you entertain Dancer. I'll be with you in a minute.

[RICHARD *pulls* DIANNE *aside.*]

RICHARD: Look, he's here . . . The boy is in the kitchen.

DIANNE: What boy?

RICHARD: Khan. He's Vietnamese. He came this morning and John threw him out.

DIANNE: Here? In the house? Oh God . . . The same one?

RICHARD: I knew him as a child; his father worked with us. He came to get some photographs, that's all. He's a good kid.

DIANNE: You don't have to convince me, but what are you going to say to John? What'll we do?

RICHARD: I'm sorry, but you'll have to talk to him. He won't take it from me. Just tell him. Khan is in the kitchen but he's leaving straight away. I don't want any trouble.

DIANNE: All right, all right . . . [*Calling*] Dancer, will you give Richard a hand for a minute?

DANCER: No worries.

DIANNE: Through there.

> [DANCER *exits after* RICHARD, *pinching* DIANNE's *bottom on the way out.*]

JOHN: [*to* DIANNE] What's going on?

DIANNE: [*crossing to* JOHN] I want you to sit down and listen to me.

> [*Silence.*]

JOHN: What's he done?

> [*Silence.*]

DIANNE: You remember that boy who came this morning?

JOHN: Sure . . . Fucking fish-head.

DIANNE: Well, it turns out—

JOHN: [*interrupting*] Poxy, slant-eyed, lying . . .

DIANNE: Listen to me!

JOHN: Yeah, yeah, yeah.

DIANNE: He came back, looking for Richard. Richard recognised him; apparently his father was a friend of Richard's.

JOHN: What a load of crap!

DIANNE: He's in the kitchen now, but he's not staying long.

JOHN: You're right, he's not, love!

DIANNE: He's catching the next train.

JOHN: He's going now.

DIANNE: Now, when he walks through that door—

JOHN: [*interrupting*] He's on his way out.

DIANNE: Yes! But, please, don't do your block.

JOHN: I won't.

> [DIANNE *signals* RICHARD *to come back in. The three enter. Silence.*
> DANCER *is enjoying the situation.*]

RICHARD: Everybody . . . this is Khan.

> [*Silence.* DIANNE *bows nervously to* KHAN.]

DANCER: Can I get anyone a drink? Dianne, a Port?

> [DIANNE *nods.*]

> [*To* KHAN] Want a tinney? Some good Aussie beer!

> [KHAN *shakes his head.* DIANNE *becomes the hostess.*]

DIANNE: How do you do? I'm Dianne.

KHAN: You are very beautiful.

DIANNE: [*to* JOHN] He's got good taste.

JOHN: You said he was leaving. He's not sitting down and having a beer
now, is he?

> [RICHARD *crosses to the bar, leaving* KHAN *at the other end of the
> room.*]

RICHARD: John, this is Khan. His father was very special to me.

JOHN: You're such a prick sometimes. Just get him out. I don't want
him in the house.

RICHARD: Hang about.

JOHN: Get rid of him.

RICHARD: You don't even know him.

JOHN: And I don't want to.

DIANNE: John, please . . .

KHAN: I have to go.

JOHN: Yes, you have to go.

RICHARD: } Wait a second.

DIANNE: } [*together*] How can you talk to him like that?

DANCER: Take it easy!

JOHN: Does he understand what I'm saying?

RICHARD: Of course he does! He can speak English! Don't treat him
like an idiot.

JOHN: Fucking fish-head.

RICHARD: He's my guest.

JOHN: Well, you get him out.

KHAN: I must go. My train is at four forty-eight.

[RICHARD *crosses back to* KHAN. DANCER *looks at his watch.*]

DANCER: Can you run fast, Khan? It's ten to five already, mate. You've missed it.

RICHARD: Jesus!

[*Silence.* RICHARD *looks to* DIANNE *for help.*]

DIANNE: [*to* KHAN] You must stay and have dinner with us.

[JOHN *looks from one to another.*]

JOHN: I don't believe this. What the hell is going on?

DIANNE: He's missed the last train.

JOHN: Look, it's my birthday and it's my house. He's bloody ruining everything. He knows! I told him this morning. This is bloody marvellous, this is! Happy birthday!

DIANNE: We can't turn him out. What's he going to do?

JOHN: Your husband's got the money to piss up every night . . .

RICHARD: That's great, coming from you.

JOHN: So he's got the money to pay for a hotel room.

DANCER: We'll do that! I'll take him with me when I leave . . . which I must do shortly.

DIANNE: Oh Johnny . . . Don't spoil everything. Now everybody wants to go. C'mon . . . just this once, let's all have dinner together . . . Please.

[JOHN *scowls. Silence.*]

JOHN: [*taking his time*] This is what I am going to do for you, Di. [*To* KHAN] You are invited to stay to my party, even though you are a [*mumbling*] fucking fish-head. You understand, don't you? We fought you in the war. I want you to know what kind of people we are. I am going to let you sit down to my birthday party. Let you see how real civilised people behave.

DIANNE: Thank you, John . . . I love you.

[DIANNE *hugs him.*]

DANCER: Beauty, mate!

[*The lights fade into blues.*]

SCENE FOUR

As the dinner scene is set up, DANCER *and* DIANNE *start dancing. The other three sit at the dinner table at the end of a meal. Miles Davis, 'Sketches in Spain', plays. At first, lights go up on* DIANNE *and* DANCER *in a slow dance as the others watch.* JOHN *sits next to* KHAN.

DANCER: She dances beautifully, your wife.

RICHARD: Yes, she does . . . my wife!

DANCER: Well, go on! You dance!

RICHARD: You O.K. over there, Khan?

> [KHAN *nods.* RICHARD *stands and* DANCER *moves back as he and* DIANNE *start to dance together.*]

JOHN: [*to* KHAN] We're all right. Aren't we, son? Let me get this straight. Your family all come over here, did they, with their jewels up their arses?

RICHARD: What's going on, eh?

JOHN: Just having a joke. Showing him the Aussie way, eh?

RICHARD: Aussie way, hell! You mean your way. Don't pay any attention to him Khan. You all right?

> [KHAN *nods and signals 'O.K.' with his fingers.*]

JOHN: I'm only having a nudge . . . Eh, Richard?

RICHARD: Yeah, O.K. [*To* KHAN] Khan, why don't you come and help me choose a record?

> [RICHARD *and* KHAN *go aside to the record collection.* DANCER *goes to the table and picks up the last of* DIANNE'S *wine.*]

DIANNE: [*to* RICHARD] There's not much wine left. I've lost my glass. [*Seeing* DANCER] Dancer!

DANCER: You're a nice girl; you shouldn't get drunk.

> [*He drains the glass.*]

Ole! Now, in Spain, when you go to the bullfights . . . [*Looking over at* KHAN] You know what they are?

> [KHAN *nods.* DANCER *takes the silver bag from the wine cask and holds it like a bag. He acts out what he describes.*]

[*To all*] They have bags of wine and they drink them like this: lift it up and squirt it . . .

> [*He squirts some wine into his mouth and laughs. He offers the bag to* JOHN.]

Here, John, you have a go, mate. You'll enjoy that!

> [JOHN *takes it and lifts it to his mouth. As he finishes, he notices* RICHARD *talking to* KHAN. DIANNE *and* DANCER *follow his gaze.* DIANNE *crosses to them.*]

RICHARD: If you want to go, just tell me and I'll take you to the hotel.

KHAN: It's O.K. All these people very nice to me.

DIANNE: Thank you. You dance with me? I'll teach you to cha cha.
[*Pulling* KHAN *into the middle of the room*] C'mon, don't be shy
. . . [*Dancing with him*] One, two, cha cha cha, one, two, cha cha cha.

[JOHN *gets up from the table and starts stamping his feet to the
rhythm behind* KHAN.]

JOHN: Yeah, shake a leg, Nigel . . . That's it mate, lift the arm . . .
Higher, higher . . .

[JOHN *suddenly makes monkey sounds, then starts to laugh.*]

RICHARD: Let me cut in, John. We'll dance in the corner over here, eh?

[RICHARD *grabs* JOHN *and pushes him into a corner.*]

That's enough, got it?

[KHAN *and* DIANNE *both stand still, looking awkward.*]

Khan, show Dianne one of your dances. A traditional dance.

[JOHN *yawns, and sits at the table.*]

DIANNE: [*to* KHAN] Go on!

RICHARD: Yeah, come on!

KHAN: No, but, if you like, I sing a song. This is about a woman
who lost her child in the war.

[*This can be told as a story or poem if the actor is unable to sing
in Vietnamese. Throughout the song,* JOHN *glares at* KHAN.]

KHAN'S SONG

[*Singing, in Vietnamese*]

This is a story about a night when there was a big noise of a bomb.
It explodes and on this night there is much blood and tears.

There is the sound of crying in the village of the poor. All the village
is on fire and the smoke rises high up to the sky.

A mother runs away from the fire with her child in her arms. She
is running from the bombs, the enemy, the soldiers, and she escapes
even though they try to stop her.

And the child is dying in her arms, but the mother does not know
this. Her child is wearing a white coat and when she arrives in a
safe place she sees the child's coat is covered in blood.

She cries, 'Who has killed my child? A thief has stolen my child's
life this night.

'What is happening to our country? My child didn't do anything
wrong.' But her sorrow is useless. The child is not there anymore,
however long she holds him in her arms.

She puts her child on the grass in the frost. 'My son didn't do anything wrong; he was too young.' She kisses her child on his forehead, on his cold body.

She touches him once, before she leaves her child forever.

[*All except* JOHN *applaud. He has closed his eyes and is slumped in his chair.*]

DIANNE: That was lovely.

DANCER: He's great entertainment value, this bloke. If you need a manager, look me up.

DIANNE: Everyone for coffee?

[DANCER *nods.*]

Come and give me a hand, sweetheart.

[DIANNE *mouths 'cake' to him in stage whisper.*]

RICHARD: Cake? I reckon he's past it.

[*He looks over at* JOHN.]

DIANNE: [*to* DANCER] We won't be a minute.

RICHARD: [*to* KHAN] That was good, mate. How about a tea?

[*He smiles at* KHAN *and puts the dog tags on the table for him.* KHAN *smiles back.*]

KHAN: Yes, please.

[DIANNE *and* RICHARD *exit.* DANCER *sits down, apart from* JOHN *and* KHAN.]

JOHN: [*with eyes still closed*] So how you going, Nigel?

KHAN: Very well, thank you.

[JOHN *opens his eyes, gets up and sits next to* KHAN.]

JOHN: Having a good night, are you?

KHAN: Yes.

JOHN: You'd better watch yourself. I've got your number, mate. I can see right through you. You know why? I have dreams about your lot. Crawly dreams . . . There's this roll of barbed wire and it stretches for thousands of miles and suddenly it starts to roll towards me and as it comes closer I see all these filthy, dirty heads, like yours, and they're laughing . . . their mouths are full of black, rotting teeth.

KHAN: Please, I don't like you talk like this.

JOHN: I don't give a shit what you like. You're in my house now.

DANCER: [*enjoying himself*] How about a beer?

JOHN: Yeah, c'mon Nigel. Let's see you drink a beer like an Aussie.

KHAN: No, thanks.

JOHN: Have a beer, don't go on about it.

[DANCER *hands* KHAN *a can of beer.*]

KHAN: I don't want it.

[JOHN *gets up, gets another beer and puts it in front of* KHAN.]

JOHN: Here we are: Crown Lager!

[*He pours a glass and passes it to* KHAN.]

This is my gift to you. I've opened the bottle, I can't do anything with it. Drink it.

KHAN: No, please. I do not drink.

JOHN: Oh, I see. You're going to waste my beer, now, are you?

KHAN: Please. It makes me feel ill.

JOHN: What are you, Nigel? A fucking sheila?

KHAN: I'm sorry. I don't mean to offend you.

JOHN: But you are bloody offending me, aren't you? You smarm up to Richard, you smarm up to Dianne. Let's give the slope a go. He's had a bad time. Let's show him some hospitality. You'll have the lease on the bloody place in a minute.

KHAN: Let me tell you this: in my country, we have a saying: Throw gold at the feet of the poor man and he will spit on it; give him a cup of water with dignity and he will be your friend.

JOHN: Well, what do you know? The little bastard's going to stand up for himself. All right, you want to get on with me? Then show some national pride: drink the beer; that's what we do in this country. And you better bloody well do it, mate, if you want to survive.

KHAN: Maybe that is what is wrong with this country.

JOHN: What is wrong with this country?

KHAN: People getting drunk to celebrate pride. This is wrong. You don't need to drink to feel good in your heart.

[JOHN *glares at him.* KHAN *takes the photographs and moves to the table.*]

DANCER: You're not going to take that, Johnny boy?

JOHN: Bastard, telling me my country's got no national pride.

[*He takes his beer and sits at the table, staring at* KHAN.]

DANCER: [*moving to the table with* JOHN] What would he know? His country's a wet stinking shithole.

[DIANNE *and* RICHARD *enter the bar area, lighting candles on a cake.*]

RICHARD: Seeing Khan today . . . remembering . . . made me realise what I've put you through. But I think from now on it can be different. I think we'll make it.

DIANNE: I hope so. That's what I want. I love you very much.

RICHARD: I love you too, so no more worrying. Perhaps you're right about another child. Just think . . . another kid in this madness.

DIANNE: Is that a promise?

RICHARD: Yeah . . . and don't worry about the photo anymore. I don't need it. I can just love her. We'll talk about it later.

[*They embrace.* DIANNE *turns to* JOHN.]

DIANNE: I've got a surprise for you, John.

JOHN: Just what I want, another surprise. Oh, look, it's a cake.

DIANNE: Make a wish.

[DIANNE *and* DANCER *start singing 'Happy birthday to you',* KHAN *joins in nervously.* JOHN *cuts the cake and it goes everywhere.*]

God you're a mess John! There's cake everywhere.

JOHN: It's bloody good. [*To* KHAN, *offering a handful of cake*] Here! Have some Australian birthday cake!

DIANNE: [*to* JOHN] Don't spill it on the floor you mongrel.

JOHN: [*gesticulating with the cake*] Have some cake! Go on!

RICHARD: Watch it!

JOHN: I'm giving him hospitality. [*To* KHAN] Go on! Have some cake!

KHAN: Thank you. I've had enough.

JOHN: Have you? That'd be right, a big feed of roast and potatoes, and now you've had enough. I'm glad you've had enough.

[RICHARD *grabs* JOHN.]

RICHARD: Leave him alone. Stop being such a prick.

[JOHN *shakes him off and glares at him. He throws the handful of cake on the table.*]

JOHN: [*to* KHAN] Enjoying the high life, eh, Nigel? Living it up at the Albury Hilton? Jeeze, I feel crook.

[JOHN *exits.*]

DANCER: That's the end of him.

DIANNE: I'm so sorry, Khan.

KHAN: I don't worry. He celebrate today.

DIANNE: Well, he'll suffer for it tomorrow.

[RICHARD *looks out after* JOHN.]

Will he be all right?

RICHARD: Yeah. He'll probably pass out. Go to sleep. [*To* KHAN] How are you feeling, mate?

KHAN: I don't let it bother me.

DIANNE: I'm so angry with him.

KHAN: I understand how he feels. He has had to fight for the other people, my people, and he is still unhappy. But it is useless to be angry. It leads only to a broken heart.

[*The actors freeze as the lights fade to blue.*]

SCENE FIVE

Lights go up on JOHN *in his bedroom.*

JOHN: You weren't much of a soldier, were you, Pixi? Always felt sick when someone was killed. And at night, when we'd lie in the shit waiting for them, you'd be scared, always shivering, like you had the cold sweats so bad. I was doing my best, holding on to you. You didn't scream. Just bit your fingers till they bled; and then you jerked up and your hands scrabbled in the dirt, throwing stones, dead leaves over your legs . . . except they weren't there anymore . . . I've got you close, mate. Can't hold you any closer. Don't go and fucking die on me, Pixi . . . You've got to get home. Promise me, you won't fucking leave me. And you know what? They don't even care. You died for nothing, mate. Nothing. Charlie got you and now he's come to get me. But we can't use mortars here. We can't keep him in his filthy, scummy streams full of mud and blood where he belongs. No. He's here. Touching my furniture, drinking out of my glasses. Eating off my plates. Smiling. You know what, Pixi? You died so that slope could come over here. You died so he could have a beer with me tonight, instead of you. That's bloody funny. Send our blokes over there and shoot them so the slopes can come back here instead. Well I'm going to even the score a bit, scare the shit out of him. You're cold aren't you, lying there in those hills? Try to sleep. I still hold you close. Remember that, mate, I'll never forget.

[*Lights fade to blue.*]

SCENE SIX

Lights go up as DANCER *pulls on his coat.* DIANNE *takes* KHAN's *hands.*

DIANNE: Your hands are freezing.

KHAN: I'm still not used to this climate.

RICHARD: It gets a bit chilly, doesn't it?

DANCER: Thanks for dinner.

RICHARD: [*to* KHAN] I'll drop you off at the hotel. I'll come around in the morning and see you, mate. Drop these photos in.

DIANNE: If I didn't have Richard, I'd come after you.

RICHARD: But you have got Richard!

> [KHAN *crosses to the lounge and picks up the dog tags on the table, then turns to look back at them. Behind him,* JOHN *enters with a gun in his hand. He points it at the back of* KHAN's *head.*]

DIANNE: I know.

> [DIANNE *hugs* RICHARD. *Over his shoulder she sees* JOHN *with the gun.*]

[*Softly*] Richard . . . Richard.

> [RICHARD *turns and sees* JOHN.]

RICHARD: John, put it away, mate.

> [KHAN *turns and sees the gun. He holds very still.*]

DIANNE: For Christ's sake. It's dangerous.

JOHN: I just thought that for the benefit of our South Vietnamese friend over here we could relive a few memories. Relax. Have a few laughs. Play a game of charades.

RICHARD: Put the gun away.

JOHN: Hey, here's one for you. What's this? Put your hands up, you bastard.

> [KHAN *holds his hands up.*]

South Vietnamese army getting ready for the next attack.

RICHARD: Have you gone crazy? Put the fucking gun away.

JOHN: Now what's this one? This one's easy! A lot of people got upset by this one. Ignorant bastards. [*Holding the gun close to* KHAN's *head*] Pcchow South Vietnamese General with Vietcong suspect.

DIANNE: Please, John . . . You're frightening me.

JOHN: Go on!

> [*Holding the gun at* KHAN's *head,* JOHN *drags him to the bamboo.*]

Show us how you make a bamboo trap.

> [DIANNE *goes to the phone. She watches* JOHN.]

How did you get here, you bastard? It costs a lot of money to get a ride on one of those leaking boats. What are you, a V.C. spy?

DIANNE: [*putting her hand on the phone*] So help me, John, I'm calling
the police.

JOHN: [*to* KHAN] Which of my mates did you fucking kill when you
were a kid? No, not a kid, there weren't any kids over there; just fucking
monsters with grenades.

[DIANNE *picks up the phone and dials.* DANCER *watches her with
alarm. He panics and lunges at* JOHN *from behind. As* DANCER *grabs*
JOHN'*s arm,* RICHARD *grabs him from the front.*]

[*Wrestling with them*] Fucking animals . . .

[*A shot rings out.* RICHARD *falls.* DIANNE *drops the phone.*]

DIANNE: Oh, God.

[*She crosses to* RICHARD.]

Richard!

[DANCER *moves to feel* RICHARD'*s pulse.* JOHN *lets the gun fall.*]

C'mon, sweetheart . . . C'mon . . .

DANCER: He's dead.

[DANCER *goes to* JOHN *and picks up the gun.*]

DIANNE: No!

DANCER: He's dead.

[*He puts the gun in his pocket.* KHAN *moves to the door.*]

[*To* KHAN] You get back here and sit down . . . Now!

[KHAN *moves back into the room.*]

JOHN: Oh, my God.

DANCER: [*grabbing* JOHN] Come here.

[DANCER *slaps* JOHN.]

Look at this . . . Look. You know what's going to happen to you? Now
you just listen to me. You listen fucking good and you listen fast mate.
I don't need this mess and I'm not getting roped into it.

[KHAN *starts to move to comfort* DIANNE.]

I told you to sit down.

JOHN: I didn't meant to do it. I didn't want to hurt him.

DANCER: Just shut up.

[DIANNE *starts to sob.*]

JOHN: It was an accident, mate.

DANCER: You hear what I said. You be quiet. How you got through
that bloody war amazes me if you go to pieces in an emergency.

[DIANNE *continues to sob. He grabs her.*]

You shut up. You listen to me, you're in this. Your brother is a fucked up Vietnam Vet who everyone is going to shit on. He's the one whose going to be locked up. Is that what you want, Dianne? . . . Now we're going to help him . . . aren't we?

[*He turns back to* JOHN. *He starts to get an idea going.*]

. . . O.K. Johnnie Boy. This is what happens. Someone breaks into the house and shoots Richard . . . he tries to get away, you struggle with him and the gun goes off. We're the only ones who know what happened, right?

[JOHN *looks at* KHAN.]

JOHN: What about him?

[DANCER *takes the gun out and points it at* KHAN.]

DANCER: He's the enemy. He is the intruder. This would never have happened if it hadn't been for him. You know what to do. You've done it before. It's the same game. It's either him or you [DANCER *puts the gun in* JOHN'*s hands*] but this time you've got the advantage. He's not in his jungle, he's in yours. You don't have any choice.

JOHN: It's just like before . . . you didn't have any choice there either . . .

[JOHN *brings the gun up and points it at* KHAN. *The lights fade to black.*]

THE END

Also available in the Current Theatre Series:

1983

THE FATHER WE LOVED ON A BEACH BY THE SEA — Stephen Sewell
THE KID — Michael Gow
SUNRISE — Louis Nowra
THE BUTTERFLIES OF KALIMANTAN — Jennifer Claire
NETHERWOOD — Patrick White

1984

MY NAME IS PABLO PICASSO — Mary Gage
THE BUCK STOPS HERE — Murray Oliver
CARAVAN — Donald Macdonald
US OR THEM — Ned Manning
DON JUAN — Moliere trans. by Nick Enright
THE BOILING FROG — Alison Lyssa
COUPLES/CONFESSIONS FROM THE MALE — Murray Oliver

1985

THE GOLDEN AGE — Louis Nowra
CHEAPSIDE — David Allen
SHORTS Volumes One and Two — Kathy Lette, Patricia Johnston,
    Strindberg, Chekhov, Moliere and Lissa Benyon
BEAUTLAND — Barry Dickins
HENRY AND PETER AND HENRY AND ME — George Hutchinson
MUSE OF FIRE — Nigel Krauth
HARLEQUIN SHUFFLE — Tony Strachan
TOO YOUNG FOR GHOSTS — Janis Balodis
A SPRING SONG — Ray Mathew

1986

LUCK OF THE DRAW — Rosemary John and the Murray River Performing
    Group
DREAMS IN AN EMPTY CITY — Stephen Sewell

Forthcoming titles:

MADAME MAO — Therese Radic